TICKLED PINK

2 designers
4 indie dyers
8 PINK-tastic patterns

C.C. Almon & Dami Almon

Hand Knit Designs Fueled by the Love of Coffee

Patterns and charts © 2018 C.C. Almon and Dami Almon / JavaPurl Designs
Photography © 2018 Melissa Foltz
Cat Illustrations © 2018 Julia Wardell

ISBN: 978-0-9935586-2-7

All rights reserved. No portion of this book may be reproduced or transmitted in any form or by any means, mechanical, electronic, photocopying, recording, or otherwise, without written permission from the publisher. This book is for personal, noncommercial use only.

Every effort has been made to ensure that these instructions are accurate and complete. We cannot, however, be responsible for human error, typographical mistakes, or variations in individual work.

Copy Editor: Katy Kidwell

Technical Editor: Rachel Brown

Models: C.C. Almon and Dami Almon

Photography: Melissa Foltz

Published by JavaPurl Designs JavaPurlDesigns.com

Printed in the USA

To the fan-freaking-tastic viewers
of the Geeky Girls Knit Podcast

and

To Pink, without which
this book wouldn't exist

contents

introduction ~ 7

easy peasy 6-colour gradient socks ~ 8

i believe in pink hat ~ 14

diamonds in the mine socks ~ 24

bashful stripes shawl ~ 32

Thistles in Bloom Socks ~ 36

Alba Cowl ~ 46

I Found Pearls in the Seaweed Socks ~ 52

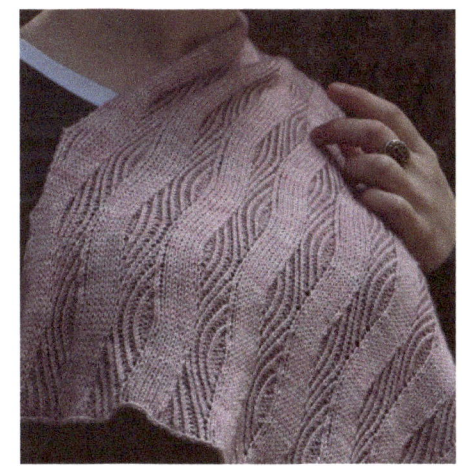
Sea & Sky Wrap ~ 62

Abbreviations/Difficulty Level ~ 68
Acknowledgements ~ 71
About C.C. and Dami ~ 74

Introduction

We're the Mamma/daughter team behind JavaPurl Designs and the Geeky Girls Knit video podcast. C.C. has been designing since 2013 and Dami has been designing since 2016. Our pattern design inspirations range from geeky things like Doctor Who and Elementary, to coffee, to colourways that demanded to be something, to the city of Edinburgh, and more.

For over a decade, I (C.C.) have had a love affair with the colour pink. After our first two books, which were inspired by coffee, we felt we had run out of coffee inspired ideas. So where else would we turn for inspiration besides the colour pink?

We love knitting with yarn dyed by indie dyers, and we wanted to highlight some of their beautiful yarns in this book. So we asked four indie dyers (Neighborhood Fiber Co., Suburban Stitcher, Abstract Fiber, and Seven Sisters Arts) to each dye up a pink colourway. Our only instruction was that the yarn had to have pink in it.

We knew each dyer's yarn would inspire us in different ways. So one of us designed a sock pattern and the other designed an accessory pattern (hat, shawl, cowl, and wrap) inspired by the same colourway of yarn.

We hope that these pink-tastic inspired patterns fulfil your knitting desires, whatever shade of pink you prefer. So grab your needles, your yarn, and let's cast on some pink yarn!

Happy Knitting!
C.C. & Dami

Easy Peasy 6-Colour Gradient Socks

by Dami Almon

Bought a beautiful gradient set of yarn at a festival and have no idea what to do with it? Trying to find the perfect pattern for that set of mini-skeins that's been in your stash forever? Look no further than these easy peasy 6-colour gradient socks!

With instructions so simple that your socks will fly right off the needles, you can use your favourite colours to create a perfectly matching pair of socks!

So grab your mini-skeins and your needles and let's get started! Happy Knitting!

Sizing: Small (Medium, Large)
To fit foot circumference: 7 (8, 9)" / 17.75 (20.25, 23)cm

Gauge: 32 sts + 48 rnds = 4" / 10cm in stockinette stitch (blocked)

Needle: US1.5 (2.5mm) or size needed to get gauge

Yarn: approximately 120 grams (500 yds / 460 m) of a fingering weight yarn | Sample is knit in Neighborhood Fiber Co. Rustic Fingering in the Roland Park & Shades of Magenta Gradient set colourways | See Yarn Notes below for more information and to help you label your yarn.

Pattern Notes:
- Pattern is written for magic loop.
- Read the pattern in its entirety before beginning so you don't miss important details.
- Instructions which are different for the 64 and 72 st patterns will be in parentheses () separated by a comma.
- Instructions in between asterisks * * are to be repeated as notated.
- Yarn Notes: You will need approximately 20 grams (85 yds / 78 m) each of six separate colourways of yarn for both socks. This is an overestimate, so you should have yarn leftover. Label the yarn for the toes, heels, and cuffs as the "main colour;" it should be a neutral. The yarns for the foot and leg should be a gradient; label them from lightest to darkest: A, B, C, D, & E.
- Abbreviations can be found on page 68.

Difficulty Level:

TOE-UP PATTERN:

Toe:
With your main colour, cast on 8 (10, 12) sts per needle using Judy's Magic Cast-On.

Set-up Rnd: K8 (10, 12), k8tbl (10, 12).
Rnd 1: *K1, M1R, k to last st on needle, M1L, k1*. Repeat on N2.
Rnd 2: Knit.

Repeat Rnds 1 and 2 until there are 28 (32, 36) sts on each needle - 56 (64, 72) sts total - ending with Rnd 2.

Foot:
Colours for the foot and leg will be worked in this order: A, B, C, D, E, D, C, B, A, B, C... etc. When instructions say to change to the next colour, move to the next colour in the pattern.

With next colour, knit 2 rnds.
With next colour, knit 4 rnds.
With next colour, knit 6 rnds.
With next colour, knit 8 rnds.
With next colour, knit 10 rnds.

Repeat this pattern, simultaneously repeating the changing colours, until your sock measures 1.5 (2, 2.25)" / 4 (5, 6)cm less than the desired total foot length, ending with the last row of a stripe. On your final rnd, stop at the end of N1.

Heel:
Change to your main colour. For this section, you will be working with the sts on N2.

Row 1 (RS): K to 2 sts before end, w+t.
Row 2 (WS): P to 2 sts before end, w+t.
Row 3: K to 1 st before wrapped st, w+t.
Row 4: P to 1 st before wrapped st, w+t.
Repeat Rows 3 and 4 until 10 sts remain unwrapped in the middle of N2, ending with Row 4.
Row 5: K10, k8 (10, 12) sts picking up the wrap with each st, w+t last st.
Row 6: P18 (20, 22), p8 (10, 12) sts picking up the wrap with each st, w+t last st.
Row 7: K18 (20, 22), w+t.
Row 8: P10, w+t.
Row 9: K to wrapped st, k wrapped st picking up the wrap with it, w+t.
Row 10: P to wrapped st, p wrapped st picking up the wrap with it, w+t.
Repeat Rows 9 and 10 until 2 wrapped sts remain on either end of N2, ending with Row 10.
Row 11: K to wrapped sts, k wrapped sts with their wraps. DO NOT TURN!

You will now have 2 wrapped sts at the beginning of N2. Begin working in the rnd, and on your next rnd (the first rnd of the leg), as you come to the wrapped sts, work the wrapped sts with their wraps.

Leg:
You will now return to working in the rnd. You need to begin with the colour and set of rnds

after the one you stopped with before starting the heel.

Work the instructions from the foot for the entirety of the leg. Continue repeating the pattern until your sock leg is desired length minus about 1" / 2.5cm for the cuff, preferably ending with Colour A.

Cuff:
Change to your main colour.
Tip: if you don't want oddly coloured purl bumps in your cuff, knit 1 rnd in your main colour before moving to the Cuff Rnd.

Cuff Rnd: *K1tbl, p1*. Work Cuff Rnd for 1" / 2.5cm or desired length.

Finishing:
Bind off using Jeny's Surprisingly Stretchy bind off. Weave in ends. And done! Except for the 2nd sock that is. Block. Wear. Enjoy!

CUFF-DOWN PATTERN

Cuff:
With your main colour, cast on 56 (64, 72) sts using a loose cast-on such as the German Twisted Cast-On. Join to work in the round.

Cuff Rnd: *K1tbl, p1* Work Cuff Rnd for 1" / 2.5cm or desired length.

Tip: if you don't want oddly coloured purl bumps in your cuff, knit 1 rnd in your main colour before moving on to the leg.

Leg:
Colours for the foot and leg will be worked in this order: A, B, C, D, E, D, C, B, A, B, C... etc.

When instructions say to change to the next colour, move to the next colour in the pattern.

With next colour, knit 2 rnds.
With next colour, knit 4 rnds.
With next colour, knit 6 rnds.
With next colour, knit 8 rnds.
With next colour, knit 10 rnds.

Repeat this pattern, simultaneously repeating the changing colours, until your sock leg measures desired leg length minus 1.5 (2, 2.25)" / 4 (5, 6)cm for the heel. On your final rnd, stop at the end of N1.

Heel:

Change to your main colour. For this section, you will be working with the sts on N2.

Row 1 (RS): K to 2 sts before end, w+t.
Row 2 (WS): P to 2 sts before end, w+t.
Row 3: K to 1 st before wrapped st, w+t.
Row 4: P to 1 st before wrapped st, w+t.
Repeat Rows 3 and 4 until 10 sts remain unwrapped in the middle of N2, ending with Row 4.
Row 5: K10, k8 (10, 12) sts picking up the wrap with each st, w+t last st.
Row 6: P18 (20, 22), p8 (10, 12) sts picking up the wrap with each st, w+t last st.
Row 7: K18 (20, 22), w+t.
Row 8: P10, w+t.
Row 9: K to wrapped st, k wrapped st picking up the wrap with it, w+t.
Row 10: P to wrapped st, p wrapped st picking up the wrap with it, w+t.
Repeat Rows 9 and 10 until 2 wrapped sts remain on either ends of N2, ending with Row 10.
Row 11: K to wrapped sts, k wrapped sts with their wraps. DO NOT TURN!

You will now have 2 wrapped sts at the beginning of N2. Begin working in the rnd, and on your next rnd (the first rnd of the foot), as you come to the wrapped sts, work the wrapped sts with their wraps.

Foot:

You will now return to working in the rnd. You need to begin with the colour and set of rnds after the one you stopped with before starting the heel.

Work the instructions from the foot for the entirety of the leg. Continue repeating the pattern until your sock foot measures 1.75 (2.5, 3)" /4.5 (6.5, 7.5)cm less than your desired foot length, preferably ending with Colour A.

Toe:

Change to your main colour.
Rnd 1:
N1 - K1, ssk, k to last 3 sts on needle, k2tog, k1.
N2 – Repeat N1 instructions.
Rnd 2: Knit.

Repeat Rnds 1 and 2 until there are 22 sts on each needle (44 sts total) ending with Rnd 2. Repeat Rnd 1 only until there are 8 (10, 12) sts on each needle - 16 (20, 24) sts total.

Finishing:

Kitchener stitch the toe. Weave in ends. And done! Except for the 2nd sock that is. Block. Wear. Enjoy!

13

I Believe in Pink Hat

by C.C. Almon

The incomparable Audrey Hepburn once said, "I believe in pink." I couldn't agree more!

For this pattern, I've taken Hepburn's quote & transformed it into a hat. Well, actually two hats. You can take your pick of having the quote circle the hat or stacking the words on top of each other. Or knit both!

So grab your yarn and your needles, and cast on your hat. I believe in pink & I hope you do too! Happy Knitting!

Sizing: Adult | To fit head circumference: 20" / 50.75cm

Gauge: 31 sts + 40 rnds = 4" / 10cm in stockinette stitch (blocked) on larger needles

Needle: US2 (2.75mm) and US3 (3.25mm) or size needed to get gauge

Yarn: approximately 108 grams (450 yds / 411 m) of a fingering weight yarn | Sample is knit in Neighborhood Fiber Co. Rustic Fingering in the Roland Park & Shades of Magenta Gradient set colourways | This yardage does not include yarn to make a pom-pom. | See Yarn Notes below for more information and to help you label your yarn.

Pattern Notes:
- Pattern is written for magic loop.
- Read the pattern in its entirety before beginning so you don't miss important details.
- Instructions in between asterisks * * are to be repeated as notated.
- Yarn Notes: You will need approximately 18 grams (75 yds / 69 m) each of six separate colourways of yarn for one hat. This is an overestimate, so you should have yarn leftover. Label the yarn for the lettering as the "main colour;" it should be a neutral. The yarns for the remainder of the hat should be a gradient; label them from lightest to darkest: A, B, C, D, & E.
- Abbreviations can be found on page 68.

Difficulty Level:

VERSION A PATTERN:

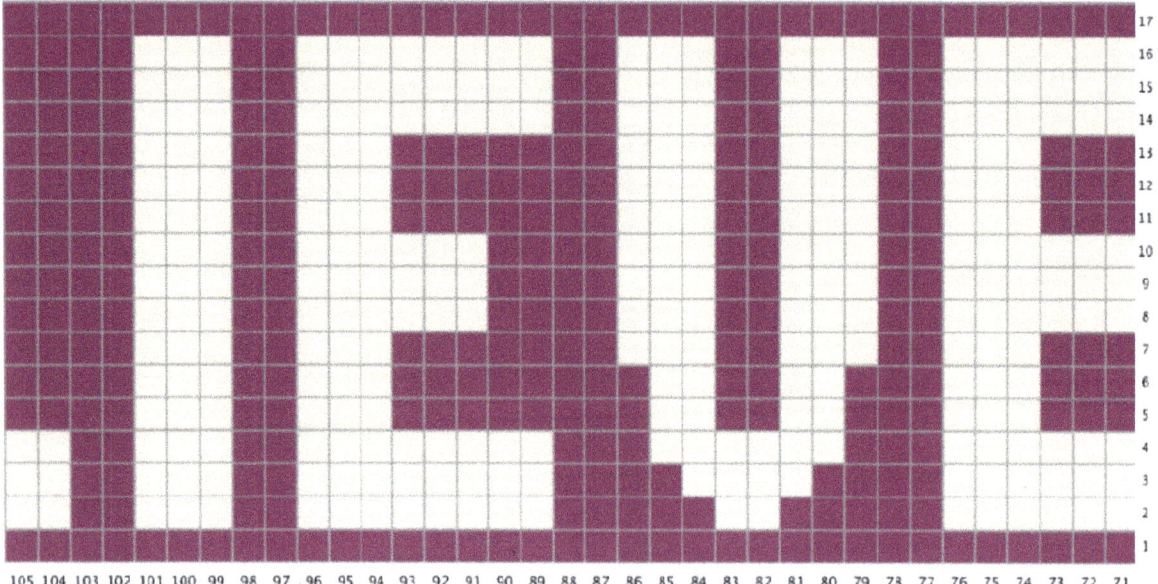

Cast-On:
Cast on 140 sts in Colour E using the German Twisted Cast-On on smaller needles. Join to knit in the round.

Ribbing:
Work 10 rnds of *k1tbl, p1*.

Body:
Change to larger needles. Knit 7 stockinette rnds. Cut yarn.

In Colour D, knit 17 stockinette rnds. Cut yarn.

In Colour C and the main colour, work the 17 rnds of the chart (use Colour C for the pink squares and the main colour for the white squares). Start with the top chart and continue to the bottom chart for each rnd (the charts were separated to make them larger and easier to follow). Cut yarns.

In Colour B, knit 10 stockinette rnds.
Rnd 11: *K14, PM* ten times.
Rnds 12, 14, + 16: *K to 2 sts before M, k2tog* ten times.
Rnds 13, 15, + 17: Knit.
Cut yarn after Rnd 17.

In Colour A,
Rnds 1, 3, 5, 7, 9, 11, + 13: *K to 2 sts before M, k2tog* ten times.
Rnds 2, 4, 6, 8, 10, 12, + 14: Knit.
Rnds 15 + 16: *K to 2 sts before M, k2tog* ten times.
Rnd 17: K2tog around.
Cut yarn.

Finishing:
Thread tail through the remaining sts and pull tight to close. Weave in ends. And done! Block. Wear. Enjoy! An optional pom-pom can be made using any one of the 6 colours or all 6 colours held together.

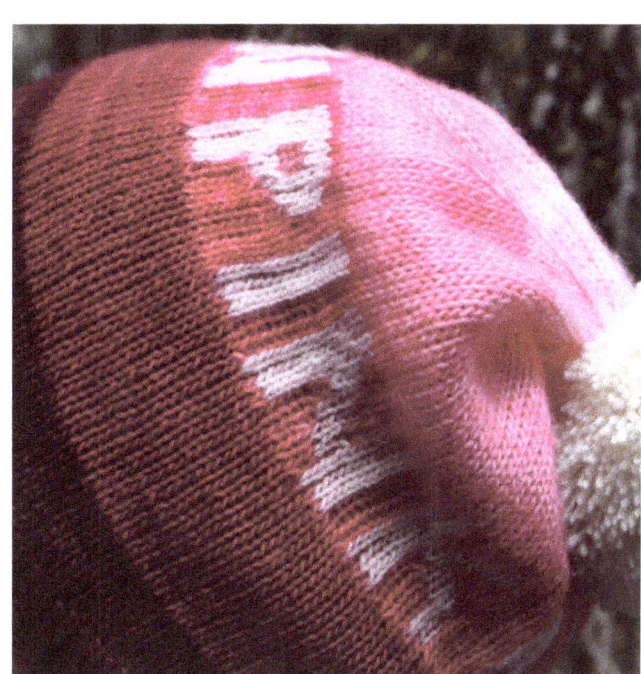

Version B Pattern:

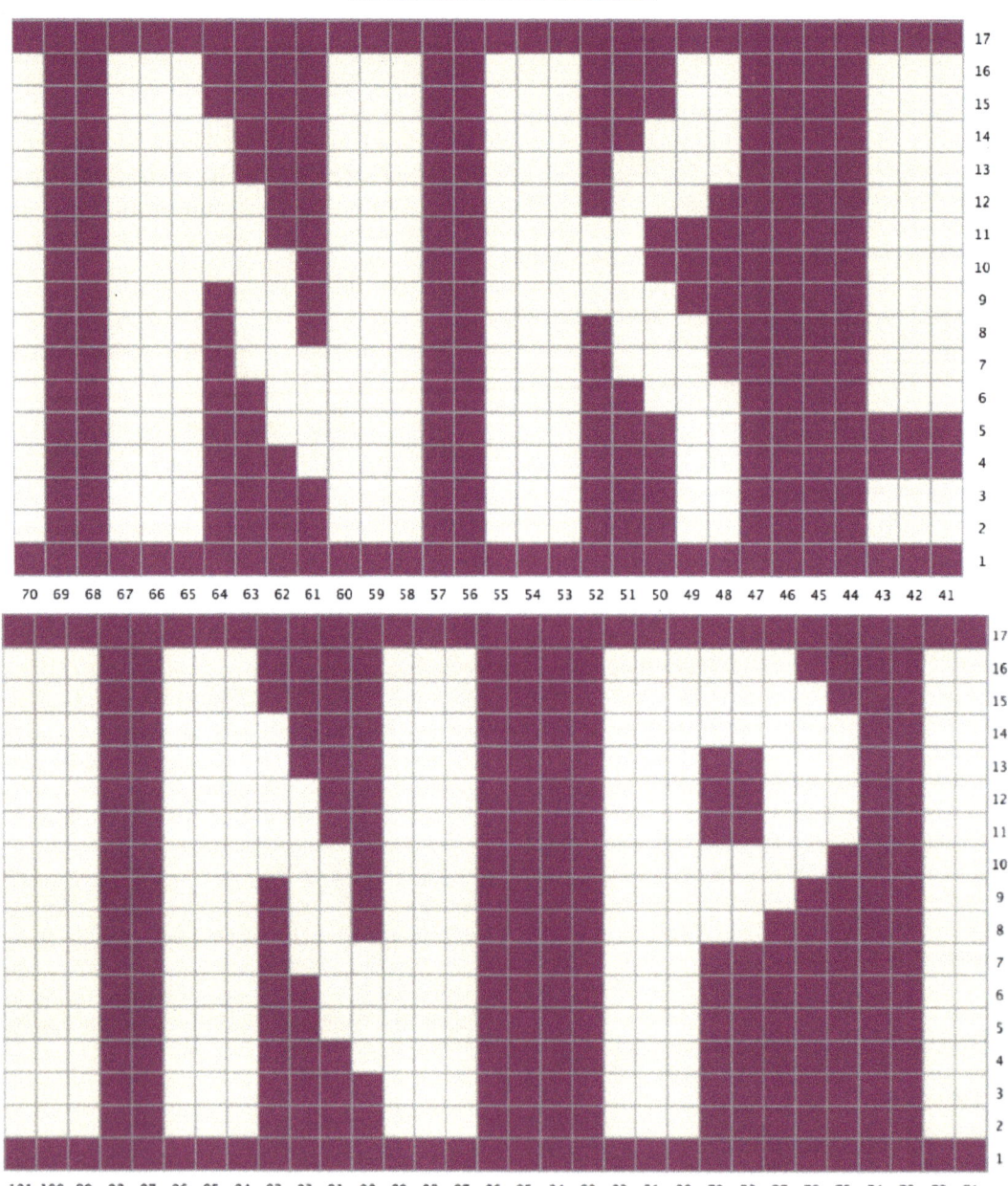

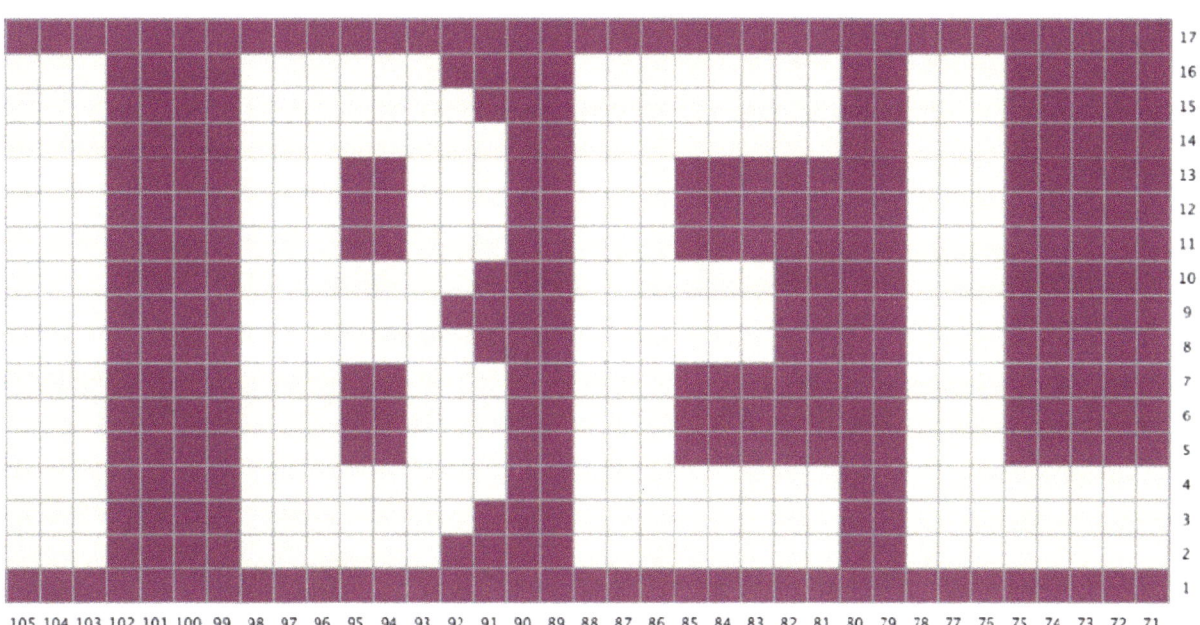

Cast-On:
Cast on 140 sts in Colour E using the German Twisted Cast-On on smaller needles. Join to knit in the round.

Ribbing:
Work 10 rnds of *k1tbl, p1*.

Body:
Change to larger needles. Knit 7 stockinette rnds. Cut yarn.

In Colour B and the main colour carrying the unused colours around the entirety of the stripe, k40 in colour B, work the 17 rnds of the IN PINK! chart (use Colour B for the pink squares and the main colour for the white squares), k39 in colour B. Cut Colour B yarn.

In Colour C and the main colour, k35 in colour C, work the 17 rnds of the I BELIEVE chart (use Colour C for the pink squares and the main colour for the white squares), k35 in colour C.

Cut yarns.

In Colour D, knit 10 stockinette rnds.
Rnd 11: *K14, PM* ten times.
Rnds 12, 14, + 16: *K to 2 sts before M, k2tog* ten times.
Rnds 13, 15, + 17: Knit.
Cut yarn after Rnd 17.

In Colour E,
Rnds 1, 3, 5, 7, 9, 11, + 13: *K to 2 sts before M, k2tog* ten times.
Rnds 2, 4, 6, 8, 10, 12, + 14: Knit.
Rnds 15 + 16: *K to 2 sts before M, k2tog* ten times.
Rnd 17: K2tog around.
Cut yarn.

Finishing:
Thread tail through the remaining sts and pull tight to close. Weave in ends. And done! Block. Wear. Enjoy! An optional pom-pom can be made using any one of the 6 colours or all 6 colours held together.

Diamonds in the Mine Socks

by Dami Almon

Diamonds don't shine, unlike what the popular song says; they reflect. You can see a whole myriad of colours in their smooth surfaces.

These dainty diamond socks can be knit in an entire rainbow of colours, from the most bashful pink to the most scandalous red.

So grab your yarn and your needles, and cast on your socks. Let's mine for diamonds! Heigh-ho! Happy Knitting!

Sizing: Small (Medium, Large)
To fit foot circumference: 7 (8, 9)" / 17.75 (20.25, 23)cm

Gauge: 32 sts + 48 rnds = 4" / 10cm in stitch pattern (blocked)

Needle: US1.5 (2.5mm) or size needed to get gauge

Yarn: approximately 100 grams (460 yds / 421 m) of a fingering weight yarn | Sample is knit in Suburban Stitcher Sock in the Bashful colourway

Pattern Notes:
- Pattern is written for magic loop.
- Read the pattern in its entirety before beginning so you don't miss important details.
- Instructions which are different for the 64 and 72 st patterns will be in parentheses () separated by a comma.
- The symbol Ø means there are no instructions for that size at this point, carry on to the next instruction.
- Instructions in between asterisks * * are to be repeated as notated.
- Abbreviations can be found on page 68.

Difficulty Level:

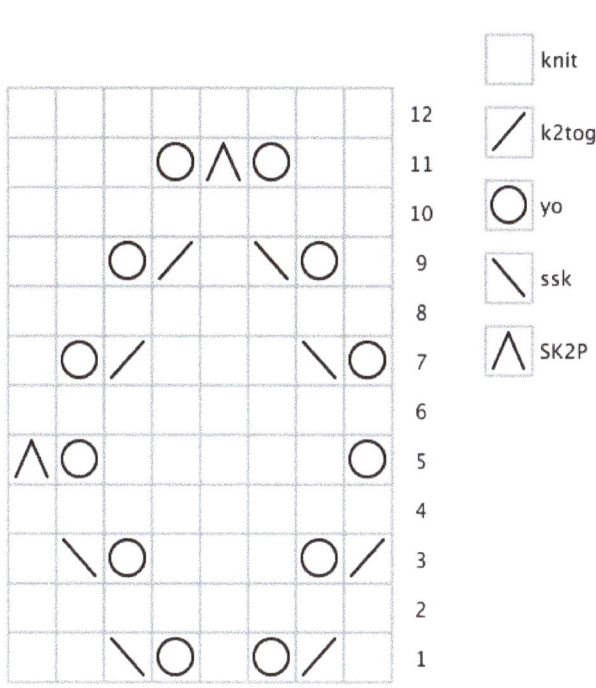

Key
- ☐ knit
- ╱ k2tog
- ○ yo
- ╲ ssk
- ∧ SK2P

TOE-UP PATTERN:

Toe:
Cast on 8 (10, 12) sts per needle using Judy's Magic Cast-On.

Set-up Rnd: K8 (10, 12), k8tbl (10, 12).

Rnd 1: *K1, M1R, k to last st on needle, M1L, k1*. Repeat on N2.
Rnd 2: Knit.

Repeat Rnds 1 and 2 until there are 28 (32, 36) sts on each needle – 56 (64, 72) sts total – ending with Rnd 2.

Foot:
N2 sts are worked in stockinette st for the entire foot.

Chart Instructions:
56 + 72 stitch:
N1 -
All Rnds EXCEPT 5 + 11: Work next rnd of chart 3 (4) times, work first four sts of chart.

Rnds 5 + 11: Work chart 3 (4) times, k4.

64 stitch:
N1 -
All Rnds: Work chart 4 times.

N2 – Knit.

Repeat Rnds 1-12 until your sock measures 1.5 (2, 2.25)" / 4 (5, 6)cm less than the desired total foot length ending with any even rnd.. On your final rnd, stop at the end of N1.

Written Instructions:
56 + 72 stitch:
N1 -
Rnd 1: *K1, k2tog, yo, k1, yo, ssk, k2* 3 (4) times, k1, k2tog, yo, k1.
Rnds 2, 4, 6, 8, 10, + 12: Knit.
Rnd 3: *K2tog, yo, k3, yo, ssk, k1* 3 (4) times, k2tog, yo, k2.
Rnd 5: *Yo, k5, yo, SK2P* 3 (4) times, k4.
Rnd 7: *Yo, ssk, k3, k2tog, yo, k1* 3 (4) times, yo, ssk, k2.
Rnd 9: *K1, yo, ssk, k1, k2tog, yo, k2* 3 (4) times, k1, yo, ssk, k1.
Rnd 11: *K2, yo, SK2P, yo, k3* 3 (4) times, k4.

64 stitch:
N1 -
Rnd 1: *K1, k2tog, yo, k1, yo, ssk, k2* 4 times.
Rnds 2, 4, 6, 8, 10, + 12: Knit.
Rnd 3: *K2tog, yo, k3, yo ssk, k1* 4 times.
Rnd 5: *Yo, k5, yo, SK2P* 4 times.
Rnd 7: *Yo, ssk, k3, k2tog, yo, k1* 4 times.
Rnd 9: *K1, yo, ssk, k1, k2tog, yo, k2* 4 times.
Rnd 11: *K2, yo, SK2P, yo, k3* 4 times.

N2 – Knit.

Repeat Rnds 1-12 until your sock measures 1.5 (2, 2.25)" / 4 (5, 6)cm less than the desired total foot length ending with any even rnd. On your final rnd, stop at the end of N1.

Heel:
For this section, you will be working with the sts on N2.

Row 1 (RS): K to 2 sts before end, w+t.
Row 2 (WS): P to 2 sts before end, w+t.
Row 3: K to 1 st before wrapped st, w+t.
Row 4: P to 1 st before wrapped st, w+t.
Repeat Rows 3 and 4 until 10 sts remain unwrapped in the middle of N2, ending with Row 4.
Row 5: K10, k8 (10, 12) sts picking up the wrap with each st, w+t last st.
Row 6: P18 (20, 22), p8 (10, 12) sts picking up the wrap with each st, w+t last st.
Row 7: K18 (20, 22), w+t.
Row 8: P10, w+t.
Row 9: K to wrapped st, k wrapped st picking up the wrap with it, w+t.
Row 10: P to wrapped st, p wrapped st picking up the wrap with it, w+t.
Repeat Rows 9 and 10 until 2 wrapped sts remain on either end of N2, ending with Row 10.
Row 11: K to wrapped sts, k wrapped sts with their wraps. DO NOT TURN!

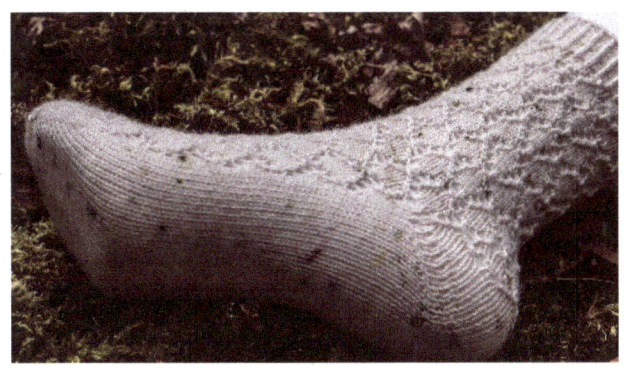

You will now have 2 wrapped sts at the beginning of N2. Begin working in the rnd, and on your next rnd (the first rnd of the leg), as you come to the wrapped sts, work the wrapped sts with their wraps.

Leg:
You will now return to working in the rnd. You need to begin with the rnd after the one you stopped with before starting the heel. Work the same rnd on N2 as you do on N1.

Chart Instructions:
All Rnds: Work chart 7 (8, 9) times.

Continue repeating Rnds 1-12 until your sock leg is desired length minus about 1" / 2.5cm for the cuff ending with any even rnd.

Written Instructions:
Rnd 1: *K1, k2tog, yo, k1, yo, ssk, k2* 7 (8, 9) times.
Rnds 2, 4, 6, 8, 10, + 12: Knit.
Rnd 3: *K2tog, yo, k3, yo, ssk, k1* 7 (8, 9) times.
Rnd 5: *Yo, k5, yo, SK2P* 7 (8, 9) times.
Rnd 7: *Yo, ssk, k3, k2tog, yo, k1* 7 (8, 9) times.
Rnd 9: *K1, yo, ssk, k1, k2tog, yo, k2* 7 (8, 9) times.
Rnd 11: *K2, yo, SK2P, yo, k3* 7 (8, 9) times.

Continue repeating Rnds 1-12 until your sock leg is desired length minus about 1" / 2.5cm for the cuff ending with any even rnd.

Cuff:
Cuff Rnd: *K1tbl, p1*.
Work Cuff Rnd for 1" / 2.5cm or desired length.

Finishing:
Bind off using Jeny's Surprisingly Stretchy bind off. Weave in ends. And done! Except for the 2nd sock that is. ;-) Block. Wear. Enjoy!

CUFF-DOWN PATTERN

Cuff:
Cast on 56 (64, 72) sts using a loose cast-on such as the German Twisted Cast-On.

Cuff Rnd: *K1tbl, p1* Work Cuff Rnd for 1" / 2.5cm or desired length.

Leg:

Chart Instructions:
All Rnds: Work chart 7 (8, 9) times.

Repeat Rnds 1-12 until your sock leg measures desired leg length minus 1.5 (2, 2.25)" / 4 (5, 6)cm for the heel ending with any even rnd. On your final rnd, stop at the end of N1.

Written Instructions:
Rnd 1: *K1, k2tog, yo, k1, yo, ssk, k2* 7 (8, 9) times.
Rnds 2, 4, 6, 8, 10, + 12: Knit.
Rnd 3: *K2tog, yo, k3, yo, ssk, k1* 7 (8, 9) times.
Rnd 5: *Yo, k5, yo, SK2P* 7 (8, 9) times.
Rnd 7: *Yo, ssk, k3, k2tog, yo, k1* 7 (8, 9) times.
Rnd 9: *K1, yo, ssk, k1, k2tog, yo, k2* 7 (8, 9) times.
Rnd 11: *K2, yo, SK2P, yo, k3* 7 (8, 9) times.

Repeat Rnds 1-12 until your sock leg measures desired leg length minus 1.5 (2, 2.25)" / 4 (5, 6)cm for the heel ending with any even rnd. On your final rnd, stop at the end of N1.

Heel:
For this section, you will be working with the sts on N2.

Row 1 (RS): K to 2 sts before end, w+t.
Row 2 (WS): P to 2 sts before end, w+t.
Row 3: K to 1 st before wrapped st, w+t.
Row 4: P to 1 st before wrapped st, w+t.
Repeat Rows 3 and 4 until 10 sts remain unwrapped in the middle of N2, ending with Row 4.
Row 5: K10, k8 (10, 12) sts picking up the wrap with each st, w+t last st.
Row 6: P18 (20, 22), p8 (10, 12) sts picking up the wrap with each st, w+t last st.
Row 7: K18 (20, 22), w+t.
Row 8: P10, w+t.
Row 9: K to wrapped st, k wrapped st picking up the wrap with it, w+t.
Row 10: P to wrapped st, p wrapped st picking up the wrap with it, w+t.
Repeat Rows 9 and 10 until 2 wrapped sts remain on either end of N2, ending with Row 10.
Row 11: K to wrapped sts, k wrapped sts with their wraps. DO NOT TURN!

You will now have 2 wrapped sts at the beginning of N2. Begin working in the rnd, and on your next rnd (the first rnd of the foot), as you come to the wrapped sts, work the wrapped sts with their wraps.

Foot:
You will now return to working in the rnd. You need to begin with the rnd after the one you stopped with before starting the heel. N2 sts are worked in stockinette st for the entire foot.

Chart Instructions:
56 + 72 stitch:
N1 -
All Rnds EXCEPT 5 + 11: Work next rnd of chart 3 (4) times, work first four sts of chart.
Rnds 5 + 11: Work chart 3 (4) times, k4.

64 stitch:
N1 -
All Rnds: Work chart 4 times.

N2 – Knit.

Continue repeating Rnds 1-12 until your sock foot measures 1.75 (2.5, 3)" /4.5 (6.5, 7.5)cm less than your desired foot length ending with any even rnd.

Written Instructions:
56 + 72 stitch:
N1 -
Rnd 1: *K1, k2tog, yo, k1, yo, ssk, k2* 3 (4) times, k1, k2tog, yo, k1.
Rnds 2, 4, 6, 8, 10, + 12: Knit.
Rnd 3: *K2tog, yo, k3, yo, ssk, k1* 3 (4) times, k2tog, yo, k2.
Rnd 5: *Yo, k5, yo, SK2P* 3 (4) times, k4.
Rnd 7: *Yo, ssk, k3, k2tog, yo, k1* 3 (4) times, yo, ssk, k2.
Rnd 9: *K1, yo, ssk, k1, k2tog, yo, k2* 3 (4) times, k1, yo, ssk, k1.
Rnd 11: *K2, yo, SK2P, yo, k3* 3 (4) times, k4.

64 stitch:
N1 -
Rnd 1: *K1, k2tog, yo, k1, yo, ssk, k2* 4 times.
Rnds 2, 4, 6, 8, 10, + 12: Knit.
Rnd 3: *K2tog, yo, k3, yo ssk, k1* 4 times.
Rnd 5: *Yo, k5, yo, SK2P* 4 times.
Rnd 7: *Yo, ssk, k3, k2tog, yo, k1* 4 times.
Rnd 9: *K1, yo, ssk, k1, k2tog, yo, k2* 4 times.

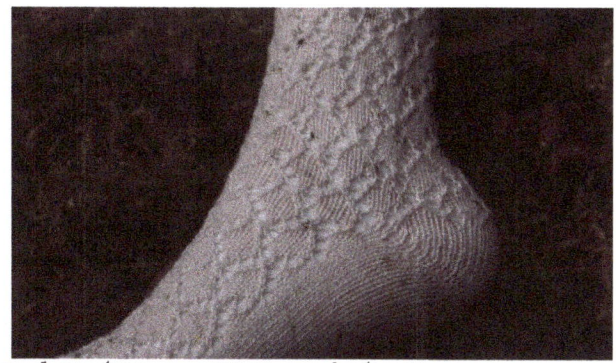

Rnd 11: *K2, yo, SK2P, yo, k3* 4 times.

N2 – Knit.

Continue repeating Rnds 1-12 until your sock foot measures 1.75 (2.5, 3)" /4.5 (6.5, 7.5)cm less than your desired foot length ending with any even rnd.

Toe:
Rnd 1:
N1 - K1, ssk, k to last 3 sts on needle, k2tog, k1.
N2 – Repeat N1 instructions.
Rnd 2: Knit.

Repeat Rnds 1 and 2 until there are 22 sts on each needle (44 sts total) ending with Rnd 2.

Repeat Rnd 1 only until there are 8 (10, 12) sts on each needle - 16 (20, 24) sts total.

Finishing:
Kitchener stitch the toe. Weave in ends. And done! Except for the 2nd sock that is. ;-) Block. Wear. Enjoy

Bashful Stripes Shawl

by C.C. Almon

When we asked Dianne of Suburban Stitcher to dye a colourway for this book, I knew whatever she came up with would be amazing. And I was right! The pale pink yarn with speckles of green, yellow, & brown is breathtaking!

The yarn may be named Bashful, but I wanted to let it speak for itself. So I paired it with Dianne's Cinder colourway for a simple garter stitch striped shawl. It's got a shallow asymmetrical shape that is perfect for wrapping up in.

So grab your yarn and your needles, and cast on your shawl. Is your yarn bashful? Happy Knitting!

Sizing: Variable depending on how many repeats you complete | Sample is 69.5" / 176.5cm tip to tip by 17" / 43.25cm tall by 43" / 109.25cm on the diagonal after blocking

Gauge: 22 sts + 44 rows = 4" / 10cm in stitch pattern but choose your needle size based on how much drape you want your shawl to have

Needle: US5 (3.75mm) or size needed to get gauge

Yarn: approximately 920 yds / 842 m of fingering weight yarn | two 100g skeins each in a different colourway | Sample is knit in Suburban Stitcher Sock in the Bashful and Cinder colourways

Pattern Notes:
- Pattern is written for knitting flat.
- Read the pattern in its entirety before beginning so you don't miss important details.
- Abbreviations can be found on page 68.

Difficulty Level:

Cast-On:
In colour A, cast on 5 sts.

Pattern Rows (for Set-Up and Sections A and B):
R1: Kfb, k to last 2 sts, k2tog.
R2: K to last st, kfb.

Set-Up: (increases st count by 20 sts)
In colour A, work R1-2 20 times.

Section A: (each full repeat of Section A increases st count by 50 sts)
In colour B, work R1-2 twice.
In colour A, work R1-2 four times.
In colour B, work R1-2 six times.
In colour A, work R1-2 eight times.
In colour B, work R1-2 six times.
In colour A, work R1-2 four times.
In colour B, work R1-2 twenty times.

PATTERN:

Section B: (each full repeat of Section B increases st count by 50 sts)
In colour A, work R1-2 twice.
In colour B, work R1-2 four times.
In colour A, work R1-2 six times.
In colour B, work R1-2 eight times.
In colour A, work R1-2 six times.
In colour B, work R1-2 four times.
In colour A, work R1-2 twenty times.

Continue repeating Sections A and B until the shawl is your desired size or you don't have enough yarn to complete another Section, ending at the end of either Section A or B.

Bind-Off:
Holding the colour you finished with doubled, bind off loosely.

Finishing:
Weave in ends. Block. Wear. Enjoy!

Thistles in Bloom Socks

by C.C. Almon

Having lived in Scotland for almost 4 years, I'm well acquainted with the beautiful thistle. Even after being back in the US for the past 9 months, I immediately pictured fields of thistles when I saw this yarn.

This sock has lace panels of blooming thistles interspersed with garter ridges that represent the fields of green grass where thistles are typically found.

So grab your yarn and needles, and cast on your socks. Let's imagine we're in Scotland! Happy Knitting!

Sizing: Women's Small (Medium, Large)
To fit foot circumference: 7 (8, 9)" / 17.75 (20.25, 23)cm

Gauge: 32 sts + 48 rnds = 4" / 10cm in foot stitch pattern (blocked)

Needle: US1.5 (2.5mm) or size needed to get gauge

Yarn: approximately 437 yds / 400 m of fingering weight yarn |
Sample is knit in Abstract Fiber Super Sock+ in the Thistle colourway

Pattern Notes:
- Pattern is written for magic loop.
- Read the pattern in its entirety before beginning so you don't miss important details.
- Instructions which are different for the 64 and 72 st patterns will be in parentheses () separated by a comma.
- The symbol Ø means there are no instructions for that size at this point, carry on to the next instruction.
- Instructions in between asterisks * * are to be repeated as notated.
- Abbreviations can be found on page 68.

Difficulty Level:

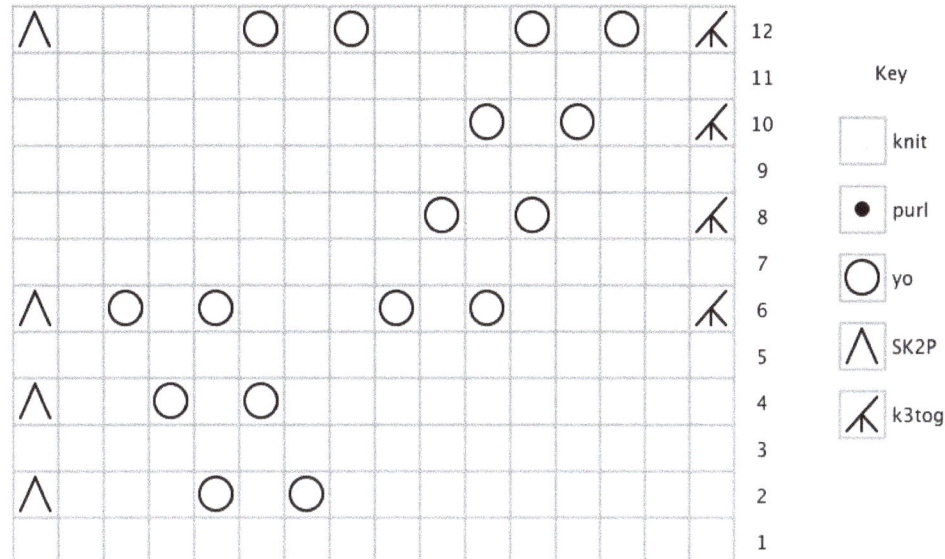

TOE-UP PATTERN:

Toe:
Cast on 8 (10, 12) sts per needle using Judy's Magic Cast-On.

Set-up Rnd: K8 (10, 12), k8tbl (10, 12).

Rnd 1: *K1, M1R, k to last st on needle, M1L, k1*. Repeat on N2.
Rnd 2: Knit.

Repeat Rnds 1 and 2 until there are 28 (32, 36) sts on each needle - 56 (64, 72) sts total - ending with Rnd 2.

Foot:
N2 sts are worked in stockinette st for the entire foot.

Chart Instructions:
N1 -
56 st -
Rnds 1-5 & 8-12: P3, work next rnd of chart, p2, repeat the first 7 sts of next rnd of chart.
Rnd 6: Sl1 from the beginning of N2 to the end of N1 (you'll now have 29 sts on N1 and 27 sts on N2), p3, work next rnd of chart, p2, repeat the first 8 sts of next rnd of chart.
Rnd 7: Sl1 from the end of N1 to the beginning of N2 (you'll now have 28 sts on both needles) and p3, work next rnd of chart, p2, repeat the

first 7 sts of next rnd of chart.

64 & 72 st -
All Rnds: P2, work next rnd of chart, p6 (2), repeat the first 8 sts (all sts) of next rnd of chart.

N2 – Knit

Repeat Rnds 1-12 until your sock measures 1.5 (2, 2.25)" / 4 (5, 6)cm less than the desired total foot length. On your final rnd, stop at the end of N1.

<mark>Written Instructions:</mark>
N1 -
Rnds 1, 3, 5, 9, + 11: P3 (2, 2), k16, p2 (6, 2), k7 (8, 16).
Rnd 2: P3 (2, 2), k9, yo, k1, yo, k3, SK2P, p2 (6, 2), k7 (8, 9), Ø (Ø, yo), Ø (Ø, k1), Ø (Ø, yo), Ø (Ø, k3), Ø (Ø, SK2P).
Rnd 4: P3 (2, 2), k10, yo, k1, yo, k2, SK2P, p2 (6, 2), k7 (8, 10), Ø (Ø, yo), Ø (Ø, k1), Ø (Ø, yo), Ø (Ø, k2), Ø (Ø, SK2P).
Rnd 6:
56 st - Sl1 from the beginning of N2 to the end of N1 (you'll now have 29 sts on N1 and 27 sts on N2).
P3 (2, 2), k3tog, k4, yo, k1, yo, k3, *yo, k1* twice, SK2P, p2 (6, 2), k3tog, k4, yo, k1, yo, Ø (Ø, k3), Ø (Ø, yo), Ø (Ø, k1), Ø (Ø, yo), Ø (Ø, k1), Ø (Ø, SK2P).
Rnd 7:
56 st - Sl1 from the end of N1 to the beginning of N2 (you'll now have 28 sts on both needles).
P3 (2, 2), k16, p2 (6, 2), k7 (8, 16).
Rnd 8: P3 (2, 2), k3tog, k3, yo, k1, yo, k9, p2 (6, 2), k3tog, k3, yo, k1, yo, Ø (k1, k9).
Rnd 10: P3 (2, 2), k3tog, k2, yo, k1, yo, k10, p2 (6, 2), k3tog, k2, yo, k1, yo, k1 (2, 10).
Rnd 12: P3 (2, 2), k3tog, *k1, yo* twice, k3, yo, k1, yo, k4, SK2P, p2 (6, 2), k3tog, *k1, yo* twice, k2 (3, 3), Ø (Ø, yo), Ø (Ø, k1), Ø (Ø, yo), Ø (Ø, k4), Ø (Ø, SK2P).

N2 – Knit

Repeat Rnds 1-12 until your sock measures 1.5 (2, 2.25)" / 4 (5, 6)cm less than the desired total foot length. On your final rnd, stop at the end of N1. rnd. On your final rnd, stop at the end of N1.

<u>Heel</u>:
For this section, you will be working with the sts on N2.

Row 1 (RS): K to 2 sts before end, w+t.
Row 2 (WS): P to 2 sts before end, w+t.
Row 3: K to 1 st before wrapped st, w+t.
Row 4: P to 1 st before wrapped st, w+t.
Repeat Rows 3 and 4 until 10 sts remain unwrapped in the middle of N2, ending with Row 4.
Row 5: K10, k8 (10, 12) sts picking up the wrap with each st, w+t last st.
Row 6: P18 (20, 22), p8 (10, 12) sts picking up the wrap with each st, w+t last st.
Row 7: K18 (20, 22), w+t.
Row 8: P10, w+t.
Row 9: K to wrapped st, k wrapped st picking up the wrap with it, w+t.
Row 10: P to wrapped st, p wrapped st picking

up the wrap with it, w+t.
Repeat Rows 9 and 10 until 2 wrapped sts remain on either end of N2, ending with Row 10.
Row 11: K to wrapped sts, k wrapped sts with their wraps. DO NOT TURN!

You will now have 2 wrapped sts at the beginning of N2. Begin working in the rnd, and on your next rnd (the first rnd of the leg), as you come to the wrapped sts, work the wrapped sts with their wraps.

Leg:
You will now return to working in the rnd. You need to begin with the rnd after the one you stopped with before
starting the heel. Begin on the same round on N2 as you do on N1.

Chart Instructions:
N1 -
All Rnds: P3 (2, 2), work next rnd of chart, p2 (6, 2), repeat the first 7 sts (8 sts, all sts) of next rnd of chart.

N2 -
All Rnds: Ø (Ø, P2), work last 9 sts (8 sts, all sts) of next rnd of chart, p3 (5, 2), repeat the full next rnd of chart, Ø (p3, Ø).

Continue repeating Rnds 1-12 until your sock leg is desired length minus about 1" / 2.5cm for the cuff ending with any odd rnd.

Written Instructions:
Rnds 1, 3, 5, 7, 9, + 11:
N1 - P3 (2, 2), k16, p2 (6, 2), k7 (8, 16).
N2 - Ø (Ø, P2), k9 (8, 16), p3 (5, 2), k16, Ø (p3, Ø).
Rnd 2:
N1 - P3 (2, 2), k9, yo, k1, yo, k3, SK2P, p2 (6, 2), k7 (8, 9), Ø (Ø, yo), Ø (Ø, k1), Ø (Ø, yo), Ø (Ø, k3), Ø (Ø, SK2P).
N2 - Ø (Ø, P2), k2 (1, 9), yo, k1, yo, k3, SK2P, p3 (5, 2), k9, yo, k1, yo, k3, SK2P, Ø (p3, Ø).
Rnd 4:
N1 - P3 (2, 2), k10, yo, k1, yo, k2, SK2P, p2 (6, 2), k7 (8, 10), Ø (Ø, yo), Ø (Ø, k1), Ø (Ø, yo), Ø (Ø, k2), Ø (Ø, SK2P).
N2 - Ø (Ø, P2), k3 (2, 10), yo, k1, yo, k2, SK2P, p3 (5, 2), k10, yo, k1, yo, k2, SK2P, Ø (p3, Ø).
Rnd 6:
N1 - P3 (2, 2), k3tog, k4, yo, k1, yo, k3, *yo, k1* twice, SK2P, p2 (6, 2), k3tog, k4, yo, k1, Ø (yo, yo), Ø (Ø, k3), Ø (Ø, yo), Ø (Ø, k1), Ø (Ø, yo), Ø (Ø, k1), Ø (Ø, SK2P).
N2 - Ø (Ø, P2), Ø (Ø, k3tog), Ø (Ø, k4), Ø (Ø, yo), Ø (Ø, k1), yo (Ø, yo), k3, *yo, k1* twice, SK2P, p3 (5, 2), k3tog, k4, yo, k1, yo, k3, *yo, k1* twice, SK2P, Ø (p3, Ø).
Rnd 8:
N1 - P3 (2, 2), k3tog, k3, yo, k1, yo, k9, p2 (6, 2), k3tog, k3, yo, k1, Ø (yo, yo), Ø (k1, k9).
N2 - Ø (Ø, P2), Ø (Ø, k3tog), Ø (Ø, k3), Ø (Ø, yo), Ø (Ø, k1), Ø (Ø, yo), k9 (8, 9), p3 (5, 2), k3tog, k3, yo, k1, yo, k9, Ø (p3, Ø).
Rnd 10:
N1 - P3 (2, 2), k3tog, k2, yo, k1, yo, k10, p2 (6, 2), k3tog, k2, yo, k1, yo, k1 (2, 10).
N2 - Ø (Ø, P2), Ø (Ø, k3tog), Ø (Ø, k2), Ø (Ø, yo), Ø

4

(Ø, k1), Ø (Ø, yo), k9 (8, 10), p3 (5, 2), k3tog, k2, yo, k1, yo, k10, Ø (p3, Ø).
Rnd 12:
N1 - P3 (2, 2), k3tog, *k1, yo* twice, k3, yo, k1, yo, k4, SK2P, p2 (6, 2), k3tog, *k1, yo* twice, k2 (3, 3), Ø (Ø, yo), Ø (Ø, k1), Ø (Ø, yo), Ø (Ø, k4), Ø (Ø, SK2P)
N2 - Ø (Ø, P2), Ø (Ø, k3tog), Ø (Ø, k1), Ø (Ø, yo), Ø (Ø, k1), Ø (Ø, yo), k1 (Ø, 3), yo, k1, yo, k4, SK2P, p3 (5, 2), k3tog, *k1, yo* twice, k3, yo, k1, yo, k4, SK2P, Ø (p3, Ø).

Continue repeating Rnds 1-12 until your sock leg is desired length minus about 1" / 2.5cm for the cuff ending with any odd rnd.

Cuff:
Cuff Rnd: *K1tbl, p1*.
Work Cuff Rnd for 1" / 2.5cm or desired length.

Finishing:
Bind off using Jeny's Surprisingly Stretchy bind off. Weave in ends. And done! Except for the 2nd sock that is. ;-) Block. Wear. Enjoy!

CUFF-DOWN PATTERN

Cuff:
Cast on 56 (64, 72) sts using a loose cast-on such as the German Twisted Cast-On.

Cuff Rnd: *K1tbl, p1* Work Cuff Rnd for 1" / 2.5cm or desired length.

Leg:
Chart Instructions:
N1 -
All Rnds: P3 (2, 2), work next rnd of chart, p2 (6, 2), repeat the first 7 sts (8 sts, all sts) of next rnd of chart.

N2 -
All Rnds: Ø (Ø, P2), work last 9 sts (8 sts, all sts) of next rnd of chart, p3 (5, 2), repeat the full next rnd of chart, Ø (p3, Ø).

Continue repeating Rnds 1-12 until your sock leg measures desired leg length minus 1.5 (2, 2.25)" / 4 (5, 6)cm for the heel. On your final rnd, stop at the end of N1.

Written Instructions:
Rnds 1, 3, 5, 7, 9, + 11:
N1 - P3 (2, 2), k16, p2 (6, 2), k7 (8, 16).
N2 - Ø (Ø, P2), k9 (8, 16), p3 (5, 2), k16, Ø (p3, Ø).
Rnd 2:
N1 - P3 (2, 2), k9, yo, k1, yo, k3, SK2P, p2 (6, 2), k7 (8, 9), Ø (Ø, yo), Ø (Ø, k1), Ø (Ø, yo), Ø (Ø, k3), Ø (Ø, SK2P).
N2 - Ø (Ø, P2), k2 (1, 9), yo, k1, yo, k3, SK2P, p3 (5, 2), k9, yo, k1, yo, k3, SK2P, Ø (p3, Ø).
Rnd 4:
N1 - P3 (2, 2), k10, yo, k1, yo, k2, SK2P, p2 (6, 2), k7 (8, 10), Ø (Ø, yo), Ø (Ø, k1), Ø (Ø, yo), Ø (Ø, k2),

Ø (Ø, SK2P).
N2 - Ø (Ø, P2), k3 (2, 10), yo, k1, yo, k2, SK2P, p3 (5, 2), k10, yo, k1, yo, k2, SK2P, Ø (p3, Ø).

Rnd 6:
N1 - P3 (2, 2), k3tog, k4, yo, k1, yo, k3, *yo, k1* twice, SK2P, p2 (6, 2), k3tog, k4, yo, k1, Ø (yo, yo), Ø (Ø, k3), Ø (Ø, yo), Ø (Ø, k1), Ø (Ø, yo), Ø (Ø, k1), Ø (Ø, SK2P).
N2 - Ø (Ø, P2), Ø (Ø, k3tog), Ø (Ø, k4), Ø (Ø, yo), Ø (Ø, k1), yo (Ø, yo), k3, *yo, k1* twice, SK2P, p3 (5, 2), k3tog, k4, yo, k1, yo, k3, *yo, k1* twice, SK2P, Ø (p3, Ø).
Rnd 8:
N1 - P3 (2, 2), k3tog, k3, yo, k1, yo, k9, p2 (6, 2), k3tog, k3, yo, k1, Ø (yo, yo), Ø (k1, k9).
N2 - Ø (Ø, P2), Ø (Ø, k3tog), Ø (Ø, k3), Ø (Ø, yo), Ø (Ø, k1), Ø (Ø, yo), k9 (8, 9), p3 (5, 2), k3tog, k3, yo, k1, yo, k9, Ø (p3, Ø).
Rnd 10:
N1 - P3 (2, 2), k3tog, k2, yo, k1, yo, k10, p2 (6, 2), k3tog, k2, yo, k1, yo, k1 (2, 10).
N2 - Ø (Ø, P2), Ø (Ø, k3tog), Ø (Ø, k2), Ø (Ø, yo), Ø (Ø, k1), Ø (Ø, yo), k9 (8, 10), p3 (5, 2), k3tog, k2, yo, k1, yo, k10, Ø (p3, Ø).
Rnd 12:
N1 - P3 (2, 2), k3tog, *k1, yo* twice, k3, yo, k1, yo, k4, SK2P, p2 (6, 2), k3tog, *k1, yo* twice, k2 (3, 3), Ø (Ø, yo), Ø (Ø, k1), Ø (Ø, yo), Ø (Ø, k4), Ø (Ø, SK2P)
N2 - Ø (Ø, P2), Ø (Ø, k3tog), Ø (Ø, k1), Ø (Ø, yo), Ø (Ø, k1), Ø (Ø, yo), k1 (Ø, 3), yo, k1, yo, k4, SK2P, p3 (5, 2), k3tog, *k1, yo* twice, k3, yo, k1, yo, k4, SK2P, Ø (p3, Ø).

Continue repeating Rnds 1-12 until your sock leg measures desired leg length minus 1.5 (2, 2.25)" / 4 (5, 6)cm for the heel. On your final rnd, stop at the end of N1.

Heel:
For this section, you will be working with the sts on N2.

Row 1 (RS): K to 2 sts before end, w+t.
Row 2 (WS): P to 2 sts before end, w+t.
Row 3: K to 1 st before wrapped st, w+t.
Row 4: P to 1 st before wrapped st, w+t.
Repeat Rows 3 and 4 until 10 sts remain unwrapped in the middle of N2, ending with Row 4.
Row 5: K10, k8 (10, 12) sts picking up the wrap with each st, w+t last st.
Row 6: P18 (20, 22), p8 (10, 12) sts picking up the wrap with each st, w+t last st.
Row 7: K18 (20, 22), w+t.
Row 8: P10, w+t.
Row 9: K to wrapped st, k wrapped st picking up the wrap with it, w+t.
Row 10: P to wrapped st, p wrapped st picking up the wrap with it, w+t.
Repeat Rows 9 and 10 until 2 wrapped sts remain on either end of N2, ending with Row 10.
Row 11: K to wrapped sts, k wrapped sts with their wraps. DO NOT TURN!

You will now have 2 wrapped sts at the beginning of N2. Begin working in the rnd, and on your next rnd (the first rnd of the foot), as you come to the wrapped sts, work the wrapped sts with their wraps.

Foot:

You will now return to working in the rnd working the foot pattern on N1. N2 sts are worked in stockinette st for the entire foot.

Chart Instructions:
N1 -
56 st -
Rnds 1-5 & 8-12: P3, work next rnd of chart, p2, repeat the first 7 sts of next rnd of chart.
Rnd 6: Sl1 from the beginning of N2 to the end of N1 (you'll now have 29 sts on N1 and 27 sts on N2), p3, work next rnd of chart, p2, repeat the first 8 sts of next rnd of chart.
Rnd 7: Sl1 from the end of N1 to the beginning of N2 (you'll now have 28 sts on both needles) and p3, work next rnd of chart, p2, repeat the first 7 sts of next rnd of chart.

64 & 72 st -
All Rnds: P2, work next rnd of chart, p6 (2), repeat the first 8 sts (all sts) of next rnd of chart.

N2 – Knit

Continue repeating Rnds 1-12 until your sock foot measures 1.75 (2.5, 3)" /4.5 (6.5, 7.5)cm less than your desired foot length ending with any odd rnd.

Written Instructions:
N1 -
Rnds 1, 3, 5, 9, + 11: P3 (2, 2), k16, p2 (6, 2), k7 (8, 16).
Rnd 2: P3 (2, 2), k9, yo, k1, yo, k3, SK2P, p2 (6, 2), k7 (8, 9), Ø (Ø, yo), Ø (Ø, k1), Ø (Ø, yo), Ø (Ø, k3), Ø (Ø, SK2P).
Rnd 4: P3 (2, 2), k10, yo, k1, yo, k2, SK2P, p2 (6, 2), k7 (8, 10), Ø (Ø, yo), Ø (Ø, k1), Ø (Ø, yo), Ø (Ø, k2), Ø (Ø, SK2P).
Rnd 6:
56 st - Sl1 from the beginning of N2 to the end of N1 (you'll now have 29 sts on N1 and 27 sts on N2).
P3 (2, 2), k3tog, k4, yo, k1, yo, k3, *yo, k1* twice, SK2P, p2 (6, 2), k3tog, k4, yo, k1, yo, Ø (Ø, k3), Ø (Ø, yo), Ø (Ø, k1), Ø (Ø, yo), Ø (Ø, k1), Ø (Ø, SK2P).
Rnd 7:
56 st - Sl1 from the end of N1 to the beginning of N2 (you'll now have 28 sts on both needles).
P3 (2, 2), k16, p2 (6, 2), k7 (8, 16).
Rnd 8: P3 (2, 2), k3tog, k3, yo, k1, yo, k9, p2 (6, 2), k3tog, k3, yo, k1, yo, Ø (k1, k9).
Rnd 10: P3 (2, 2), k3tog, k2, yo, k1, yo, k10, p2 (6, 2), k3tog, k2, yo, k1, yo, k1 (2, 10).
Rnd 12: P3 (2, 2), k3tog, *k1, yo* twice, k3, yo, k1, yo, k4, SK2P, p2 (6, 2), k3tog, *k1, yo* twice, k2 (3, 3), Ø (Ø, yo), Ø (Ø, k1), Ø (Ø, yo), Ø (Ø, k4), Ø (Ø, SK2P).

N2 – Knit

Continue repeating Rnds 1-12 until your sock foot measures 1.75 (2.5, 3)" /4.5 (6.5, 7.5)cm less than your desired foot length ending with any odd rnd.

TOE:
Rnd 1:
N1 - K1, ssk, k to last 3 sts on needle, k2tog, k1.
N2 – Repeat N1 instructions.
Rnd 2: Knit.

Repeat Rnds 1 and 2 until there are 22 sts on each needle (44 sts total) ending with Rnd 2.

Repeat Rnd 1 only until there are 8 (10, 12) sts on each needle - 16 (20, 24) sts total.

Finishing:
Kitchener stitch the toe. Weave in ends. And done! Except for the 2nd sock that is. ;-) Block. Wear. Enjoy!

ALBA COWL

by Dami Almon

Alba is the Scottish Gaelic word for *Scotland*. Scotland is home to the beautiful (and dangerous) thistle, crisp autumn mornings, and jewel-toned sunrises and sunsets.

This cowl combines the beauty of all of Scotland's treasures into a unique slipped-stitch design, almost looking like a field of thistles when completed.

So grab your yarn and your needles, and cast on your cowl. Enjoy your Scottish adventure! Happy Knitting!

Sizing: One size, variable depending on how many repeats you complete
Sample has 2.25 repeats and is 12.5" / 31.75cm wide by 7.5" / 19cm tall (blocked)

Gauge: 28 sts + 40 rnds = 4" / 10cm in stitch pattern

Needle: US4 (3.5mm) or size needed to get gauge

Yarn: approximately 200 grams (880 yds / 805 m) of a fingering weight yarn | Sample is knit in Abstract Fiber SuperSock+ in the Thistle and Malabrigo Sock in the Fresco y Seco colourways

Pattern Notes:
- Pattern is written for magic loop.
- Read the pattern in its entirety before beginning so you don't miss important details.
- Designate your two colours A and B.
- Instructions in between asterisks * * are to be repeated as notated.
- Abbreviations can be found on page 68.

Difficulty Level:

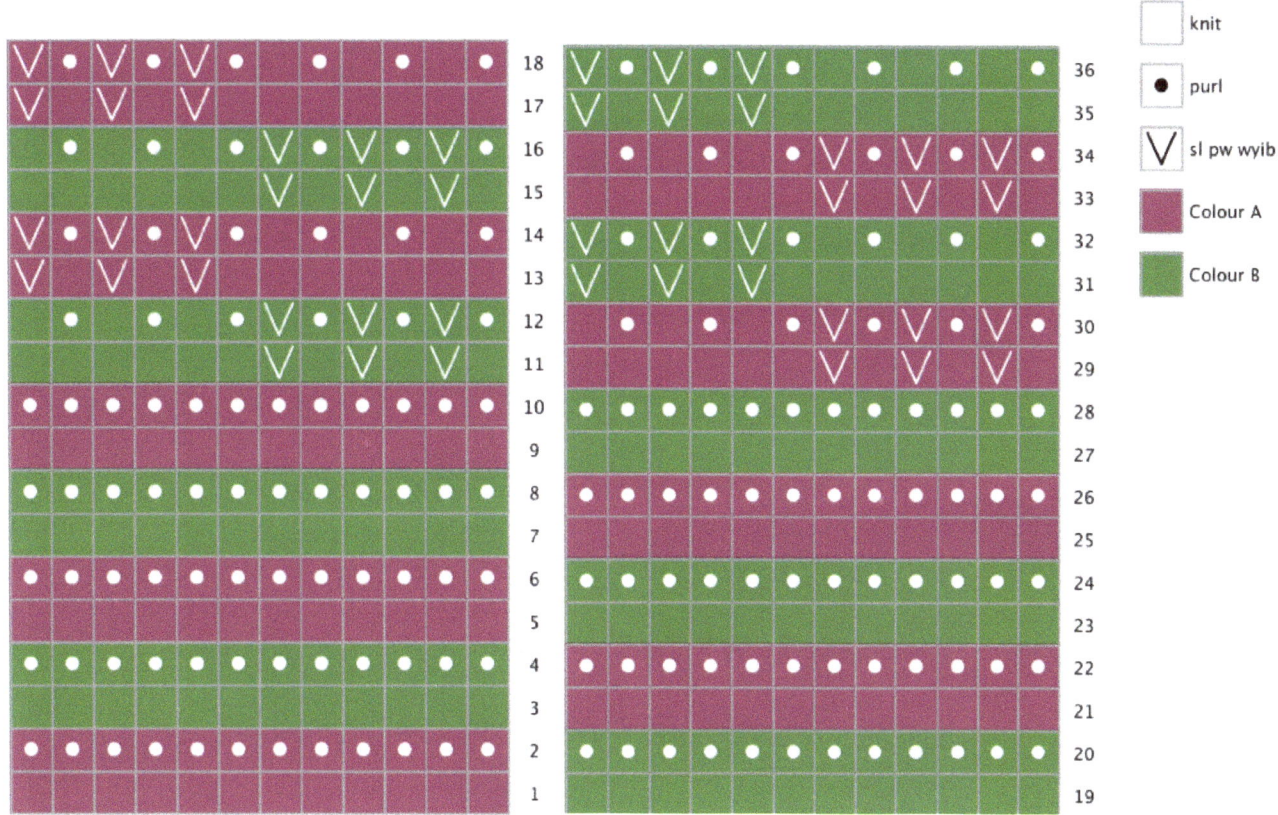

PATTERN:

Cast-On:
Cast on 180 sts with Colour B using a stretchy cast on. Join to work in the round.

Ribbing:
K1tbl, p1 for 10 rnds.

Main Pattern:
For the main pattern, you will alternate colours every two rnds, starting with Colour A (two rnds A, two rnds B, two rnds A, etc).

Chart Instructions:
Rnds 1-36: Repeat Chart 15 times.

Repeat Rnds 1-36, stopping when your cowl is desired length, preferably ending with Rnd 10.

Written Instructions:

Rnd 1 and all odd rnds through Rnd 9: Knit.
Rnd 2 and all even rnds through Rnd 10: Purl
Rnds 11 + 15: [*K1, sl1* 3 times, k6] 15 times.
Rnds 12 + 16: [*P1, sl1* 3 times, *p1, k1* 3 times] 15 times.
Rnds 13 + 17: [K6, *k1, sl1* 3 times] 15 times.
Rnds 14 + 18: [*P1, k1* 3 times, *p1, sl1* 3 times] 15 times.
Rnd 19 and all odd rnds through Rnd 27: Knit.
Rnd 20 and all even rnds through Rnd 28: Purl.
Rnds 29 + 33: [*K1, sl1* 3 times, k6] 15 times.
Rnds 30 + 34: [*P1, sl1* 3 times, *p1, k1* 3 times] 15 times.
Rnds 31 + 35: [K6, *k1, sl1* 3 times] 15 times.
Rnds 32 + 36: [*P1, k1* 3 times, *p1, sl1* 3 times] 15 times.

Repeat Rnds 1-36, stopping when your cowl is desired length, preferably ending with Rnd 10.

Ribbing:
Change to Colour B. *K1tbl, p1* for 10 rnds.

Finishing:
Bind off with a stretchy bind-off. Weave in ends. Block. Wear. Enjoy!

I Found Pearls in the Seaweed Socks

by C.C. Almon

The colourway name of this yarn, Pink Pearl, instantly made me think of the ocean since that's where saltwater pearls are found. And when I think of the ocean, I think of seaweed.

For these socks, I paired two cables. One is representative of seaweed & the other is lots of pearls stacked on top of each other.

So grab your yarn and your needles, and cast on your socks. You might find a pearl in the seaweed! Happy Knitting!

Sizing: Women's Small (Medium, Large)
To fit foot circumference: 7 (8, 9)" / 17.75 (20.25, 23)cm

Gauge: 33 sts + 43 rnds = 4" / 10cm in foot stitch pattern (blocked) on US2 (2.75mm) needles

Needle: US1.5 (2.5mm), US2 (2.75mm), and US2.5 (3mm) or size needed to get gauge

Yarn: approximately 463 yds / 423 m of fingering weight yarn |
Sample is knit in Seven Sisters Arts Meridian in the Pink Pearl colourway

Pattern Notes:

- Pattern is written for magic loop.
- Read the pattern in its entirety before beginning so you don't miss important details.
- Instructions which are different for the 64 and 72 st patterns will be in parentheses () separated by a comma.
- The symbol Ø means there are no instructions for that size at this point, carry on to the next instruction.
- Instructions in between asterisks * * are to be repeated as notated.
- Because of the cable pattern, you will need to go up 1-2 needle sizes as notated in the pattern, especially on the leg of the sock. However, make sure and try on your sock as you go to see if you need to make any needle size modifications.
- Abbreviations can be found on page 68.

Difficulty Level:

Seaweed

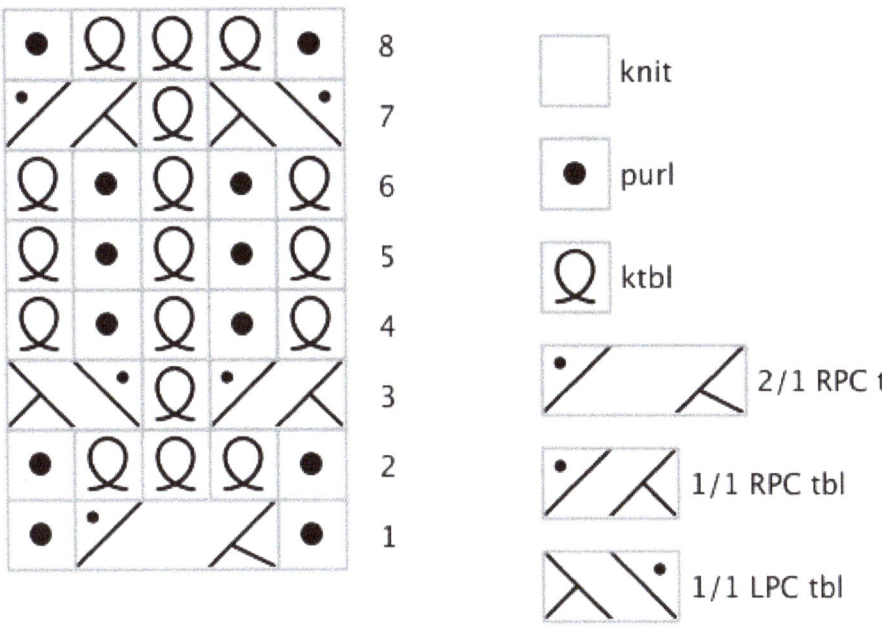

Seaweed Written Instructions:
R1: P1, 2/1 RPC tbl, p1.
R2 + 8: P1, k3tbl, p1.
R3: 1/1 RPC tbl, k1tbl, 1/1 LPC tbl.
R4, 5, + 6: *K1tbl, p1* twice, k1tbl.
R7: 1/1 LPC tbl, k1tbl, 1/1 RPC tbl.

Pearls

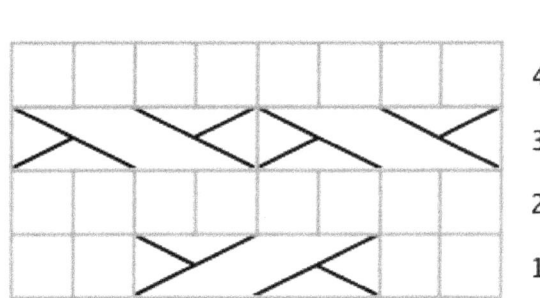

Key

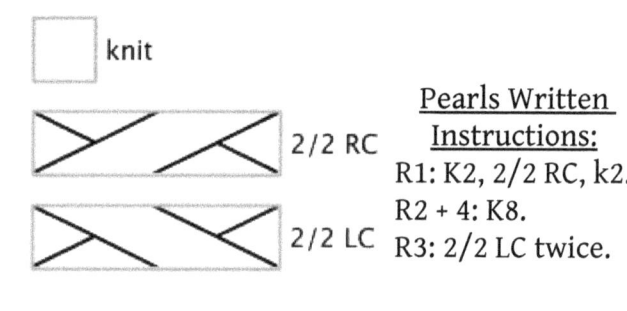

Pearls Written Instructions:
R1: K2, 2/2 RC, k2.
R2 + 4: K8.
R3: 2/2 LC twice.

Additional Abbreviations:

1/1 LPC tbl: sl1 to CN, hold in front, p1, k1tbl from CN

1/1 RPC tbl: sl1 to CN, hold in back, k1tbl, p1 from CN

2/1 RPC tbl: sl2 to CN, hold in back, k1tbl, p1, k1tbl from CN

2/2 LC: sl2 to CN, hold in front, k2, k2 from CN

2/2 RC: sl2 to CN, hold in back, k2, k2 from CN

TOE-UP PATTERN:

Toe:
On US1.5 (2.5mm) needles, cast on 8 (10, 12) sts per needle using Judy's Magic Cast-On.

Set-up Rnd: K8 (10, 12), k8tbl (10, 12).
Rnd 1: *K1, M1R, k to last st on needle, M1L, k1*. Repeat on N2.
Rnd 2: Knit.

Repeat Rnds 1 and 2 until there are 28 (32, 36) sts on each needle – 56 (64, 72) sts total - ending with Rnd 2.

Foot:

N2 sts are worked in stockinette st for the entire foot.

Change to US2 (2.75mm) needles.

Set-Up Rnd:
N1 - P5 (2, 6), k3tbl, p4, k3tbl, p3 (4, 4), Ø (k3tbl, k3tbl), Ø (p3, p3), k8, p2.
N2 – Knit.

Chart/Written Instructions:
The Pearls Chart/Written Instructions is worked twice for every one time the Seaweed Chart/Written Instructions is worked.

N1 -
All Rnds: P4 (1, 5), *work next rnd of Seaweed Chart/Written Instructions, p2* twice (three times, three times), work next rnd of Pearls Chart/Written Instructions, p2.

N2 – Knit

Repeat Rnds 1-8 until your sock measures 1.5 (2, 2.25)" / 4 (5, 6)cm less than the desired total foot length ending with an even rnd. On your final rnd, stop at the end of N1.

Heel:

For this section, you will be working with the sts on N2.

Change to US1.5 (2.5mm) needles.

Row 1 (RS): K to 2 sts before end, w+t.
Row 2 (WS): P to 2 sts before end, w+t.
Row 3: K to 1 st before wrapped st, w+t.
Row 4: P to 1 st before wrapped st, w+t.
Repeat Rows 3 and 4 until 10 sts remain unwrapped in the middle of N2, ending with Row 4.
Row 5: K10, k8 (10, 12) sts picking up the wrap with each st, w+t last st.
Row 6: P18 (20, 22), p8 (10, 12) sts picking up the wrap with each st, w+t last st.
Row 7: K18 (20, 22), w+t.
Row 8: P10, w+t.
Row 9: K to wrapped st, k wrapped st picking up the wrap with it, w+t.
Row 10: P to wrapped st, p wrapped st picking up the wrap with it, w+t.
Repeat Rows 9 and 10 until 2 wrapped sts

remain on either end of N2, ending with Row 10.
Row 11: K to wrapped sts, k wrapped sts with their wraps. DO NOT TURN!

You will now have 2 wrapped sts at the beginning of N2. Begin working in the rnd, and on your next rnd (the first rnd of the leg), as you come to the wrapped sts, work the wrapped sts with their wraps.

Leg:
You will now return to working in the rnd. You need to begin with the rnd after the one you stopped with before starting the heel. Begin on the same round on N2 as you do on N1.

Change to US2.5 (3mm) needles.

Chart/Written Instructions:
N1 -
Work the N1 instructions from the foot for the entirety of the leg.

N2 -
Work the N1 instructions from the foot for the entirety of the leg.

Continue repeating Rnds 1-8 until your sock leg is desired length minus about 1" / 2.5cm for the cuff ending with any even rnd.

Cuff:
Change to US1.5 (2.5mm) needles.

Cuff Rnd: *K1tbl, p1*.
Work Cuff Rnd for 1" / 2.5cm or desired length.

Finishing:
Bind off using Jeny's Surprisingly Stretchy bind off. Weave in ends. And done! Except for the 2nd sock that is. ;-) Block. Wear. Enjoy!

CUFF-DOWN PATTERN

Cuff:
On US1.5 (2.5mm) needles, cast on 56 (64, 72) sts using a loose cast-on such as the German Twisted Cast-On.

Cuff Rnd: *K1tbl, p1* Work Cuff Rnd for 1" / 2.5cm or desired length.

Leg:
Change to US2.5 (3mm) needles.

Set-Up Rnd:
N1 + 2 - P5 (2, 6), k3tbl, p4, k3tbl, p3 (4, 4), Ø (k3tbl, k3tbl), Ø (p3, p3), k8, p2.

Chart/Written Instructions:

The Pearls Chart/Written Instructions is worked twice for every one time the Seaweed Chart/Written Instructions is worked.

N1 and N2-
All Rnds: P4 (1, 5), *work next rnd of Seaweed Chart/Written Instructions, p2* twice (three times, three times), work next rnd of Pearls Chart/Written Instructions, p2.

Continue repeating Rnds 1-8 until your sock leg measures desired leg length minus 1.5 (2, 2.25)" / 4 (5, 6)cm for the heel. On your final rnd, stop at the end of N1.

Heel:

For this section, you will be working with the sts on N2.

Change to US1.5 (2.5mm) needles.

Row 1 (RS): K to 2 sts before end, w+t.
Row 2 (WS): P to 2 sts before end, w+t.
Row 3: K to 1 st before wrapped st, w+t.
Row 4: P to 1 st before wrapped st, w+t.
Repeat Rows 3 and 4 until 10 sts remain unwrapped in the middle of N2, ending with Row 4.
Row 5: K10, k8 (10, 12) sts picking up the wrap with each st, w+t last st.
Row 6: P18 (20, 22), p8 (10, 12) sts picking up the wrap with each st, w+t last st.
Row 7: K18 (20, 22), w+t.
Row 8: P10, w+t.
Row 9: K to wrapped st, k wrapped st picking up the wrap with it, w+t.
Row 10: P to wrapped st, p wrapped st picking up the wrap with it, w+t.
Repeat Rows 9 and 10 until 2 wrapped sts remain on either end of N2, ending with Row 10.
Row 11: K to wrapped sts, k wrapped sts with their wraps. DO NOT TURN!

You will now have 2 wrapped sts at the beginning of N2. Begin working in the rnd, and on your next rnd (the first rnd of the foot), as you come to the wrapped sts, work the wrapped sts with their wraps.

Foot:

You will now return to working in the rnd working the foot pattern on N1. N2 sts are worked in stockinette st for the entire foot.

Change to US2 (2.75mm) needles.

Chart/Written Instructions:

N1 –
Work the N1 instructions from the leg for the entirety of the foot.

N2 – Knit

Continue repeating Rnds 1-8 until your sock foot measures 1.75 (2.5, 3)" /4.5 (6.5, 7.5)cm less than your desired foot length ending with any even rnd.

Toe:
Change to US1.5 (2.5mm) needles.

Rnd 1:
N1 - K1, ssk, k to last 3 sts on needle, k2tog, k1.
N2 – Repeat N1 instructions.
Rnd 2: Knit.

Repeat Rnds 1 and 2 until there are 22 sts on each needle (44 sts total) ending with Rnd 2.

Repeat Rnd 1 only until there are 8 (10, 12) sts on each needle - 16 (20, 24) sts total.

Finishing:
Kitchener stitch the toe. Weave in ends. And done! Except for the 2nd sock that is. ;-) Block. Wear. Enjoy!

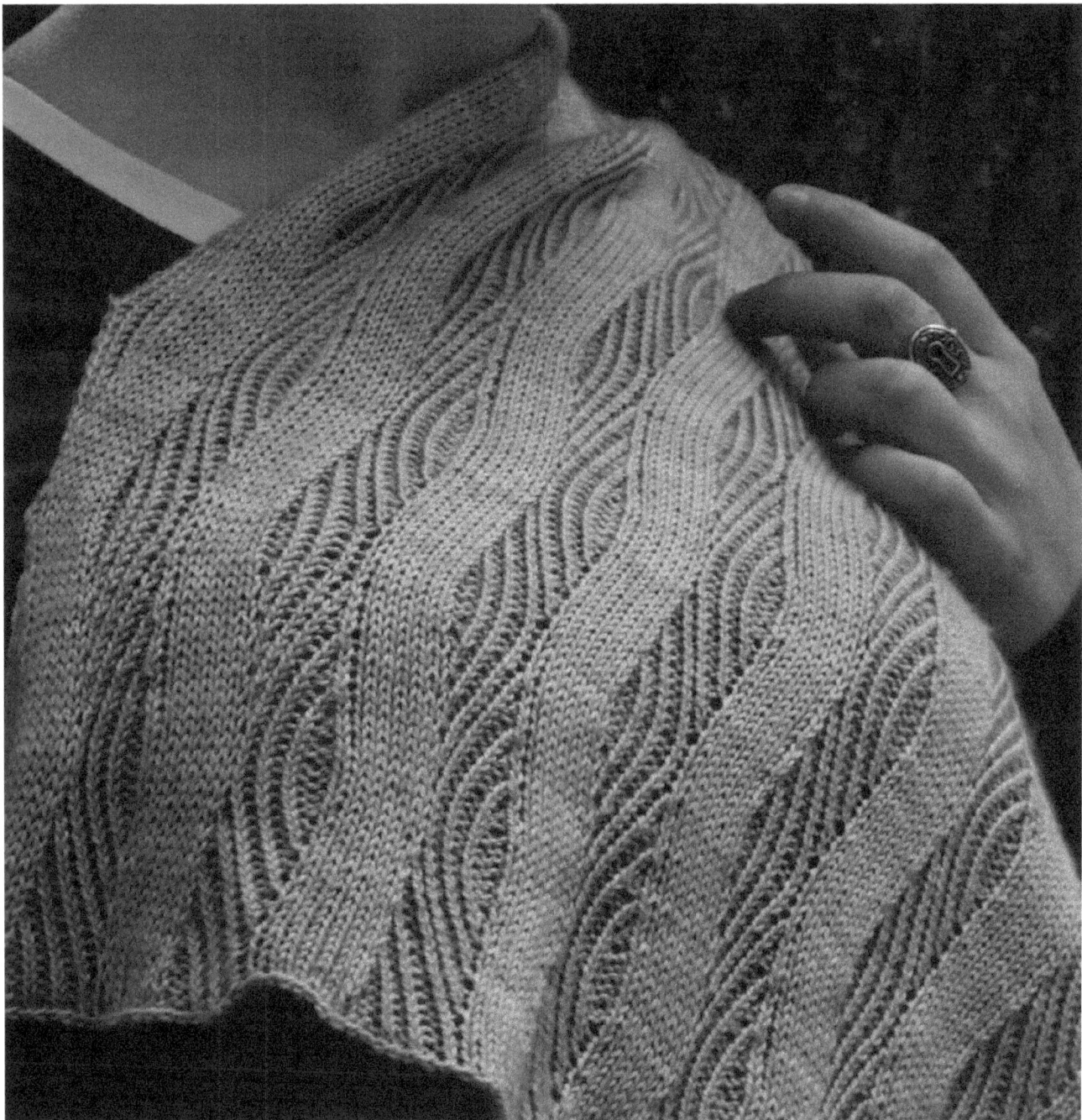

Sea & Sky Wrap

by Dami Almon

The place where sea and sky meet is called the horizon. Gazing into a tinted-pink sky at sunset, looking into the horizon, you feel as if you could see all the way to the other side of the Earth.

In this wrap, ocean waves and clouds meet multiple times to give you the sense of wrapping yourself in the warmth of a beach sunset. And if you look just far enough, you may be able to see the end of this several-foot long wrap in sight.

So grab your yarn and your needles, and cast on your wrap. Let's enjoy the beautiful sunset together. Happy Knitting!

Sizing: One size that is variable depending on how many repeats you complete | Sample has 14 repeats and is 14.5" / 36.75cm wide by 60" / 152.5cm long (blocked)

Gauge: 28 sts + 44 rows = 4" / 10cm in stitch pattern (blocked)

Needle: US3 (3.25mm) or size needed to get gauge

Yarn: approximately 200 grams (800 yds / 732 m) of fingering weight yarn | Sample is knit in Seven Sisters Arts Matrika in the Pink Pearl colourway

Pattern Notes:
- Pattern is written for knitting flat.
- Read the pattern in its entirety before beginning so you don't miss important details.
- Instructions in between asterisks * * and brackets [ ] are to be repeated as notated.
- If you'd like to make this into a skinnier scarf, cast on 14 sts (or multiples of 14 sts) less than the called for st count. Then repeat the chart/repeated instructions 1 (or the number of multiples of 14 sts) less than the pattern calls for.
- If you'd like to make this into a cowl, provisionally cast on your sts. Do not complete the set-up row. Instead start immediately with the chart/written instructions. At the end, do not knit 6 rows. Instead, graft your live sts with the provisionally cast on sts. If you'd like the cowl to be skinnier, follow the instructions above for a skinnier scarf in regards to st count.
- Abbreviations can be found on page 68.

Difficulty Level:

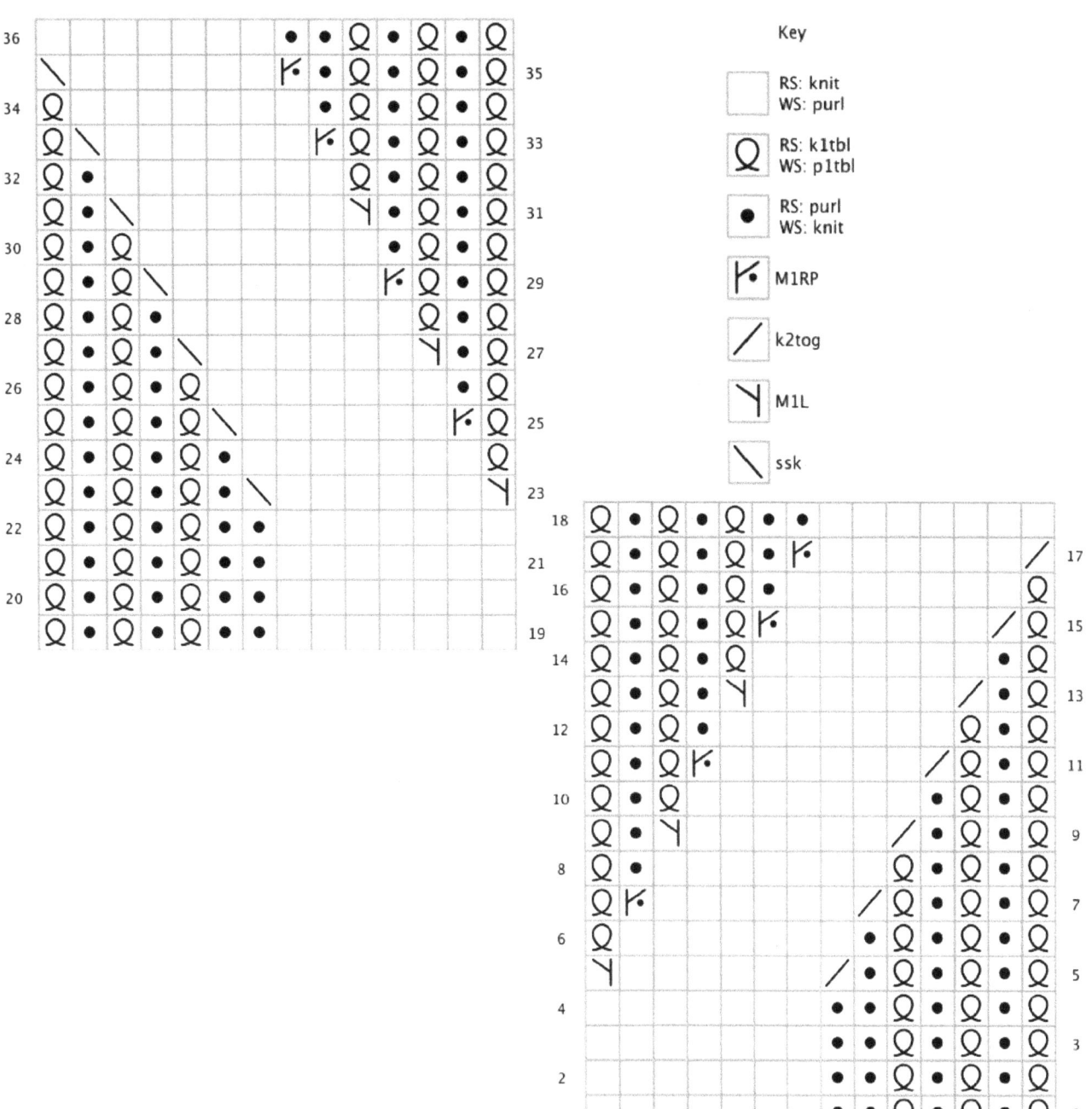

Cast-On:
Cast on 114 sts.
Set-up Row (WS): K1, p to end, k1.

Main Pattern:

Chart Instructions:
All Rows: K1, work chart as written eight times, k1.

Repeat Rows 1-36 until your wrap measures desired length, ending with R36.

Written Instructions:
R1 + 3 (RS): K1, *[k1tbl, p1] twice, k1tbl, p2, k7*

PATTERN:
eight times, k1.
R2, 4 + 36 (WS): K1, *p7, k2, p1tbl, [k1, p1tbl] twice* eight times, k1.
R5: K1, *[k1tbl, p1] 3 times, k2tog, k6, M1L* eight times, k1.
R6 + 34: K1, *p1tbl, p7, [k1, p1tbl] 3 times* eight times, k1.
R7: K1, *[k1tbl, p1] twice, k1tbl, k2tog, k6, M1RP, k1tbl* eight times, k1.
R8 + 32: K1, *p1tbl, k1, p7, p1tbl, [k1, p1tbl] twice* eight times, k1.
R9: K1, *[k1tbl, p1] twice, k2tog, k6, M1L, p1, k1tbl* eight times, k1.
R10 + 30: K1, *p1tbl, k1, p1tbl, p7, [k1, p1tbl] twice* eight times, k1.
R11: K1, *k1tbl, p1, k1tbl, k2tog, k6, M1RP, k1tbl,

p1, k1tbl* eight times, k1.
R12 + 28: K1, *[p1tbl, k1] twice, p7, p1tbl, k1, p1tbl* eight times, k1.
R13: K1, *k1tbl, p1, k2tog, k6, M1L, [p1, k1tbl] twice* eight times, k1.
R14 + 26: K1, *[p1tbl, k1] twice, p1tbl, p7, k1, p1tbl* eight times, k1.
R15: K1, *k1tbl, k2tog, k6, M1RP, [k1tbl, p1] twice, k1tbl* eight times, k1.
R16 + 24: K1, *[p1tbl, k1] 3 times, p7, p1tbl* eight times, k1.
R17: K1, *k2tog, k6, M1RP, [p1, k1tbl] 3 times* eight times, k1.
R18, 20, + 22: K1, *[p1tbl, k1] twice, p1tbl, k2, p7* eight times, k1.
R19 + 21: K1, *k7, p2, k1tbl, [p1, k1tbl] twice* eight times, k1.
R23: K1, *M1L, k6, ssk, [p1, k1tbl] 3 times* eight times, k1.
R25: K1, *k1tbl, M1RP, k6, ssk, k1tbl, [p1, k1tbl] twice* eight times, k1.
R27: K1, *k1tbl, p1, M1L, k6, ssk, [p1, k1tbl] twice* eight times, k1.
R29: K1, *k1tbl, p1, k1tbl, M1RP, k6, ssk, k1tbl, p1, k1tbl* eight times, k1.
R31: K1, *[k1tbl, p1] twice, M1L, k6, ssk, p1, k1tbl* eight times, k1.
R33: K1, *[k1tbl, p1] twice, k1tbl, M1RP, k6, ssk, k1tbl* eight times, k1.
R35: K1, *[k1tbl, p1] 3 times, M1RP, k6, ssk* eight times, k1.

Repeat Rows 1-36 until your wrap measures desired length, ending with R36.

Finishing:

Bind off loosely. Weave in ends. And done! Block. Wear. Enjoy!

Abbreviations

k	knit
k2tog	knit 2 sts together [1 st decreased]
k3tog	knit 3 sts together [2 sts decreased]
kfb	knit front and back [1 st increased]
ktbl	knit through the back loop
kw	knitwise
LH	left hand
M	marker
M1L	make 1 left (pick up strand of yarn between 2 sts from front to back and knit through the back of lifted strand) [1 st increased]
M1R	make 1 right (pick up strand of yarn between 2 sts from back to front and knit through the front of lifted strand) [1st increased]
M1RP	make 1 right purl (pick up strand of yarn between 2 sts from back to front and purl through the front of lifted strand) [1 st increased]
N	needle
p	purl
PM	place marker
ptbl	purl through back loop
pw	purlwise
R	Row
RH	right hand
rnd	Round

RS	right side
SK2P	sl1 kw, k2tog, pass slipped st over the k2tog [2 sts decreased]
sl	slip 1 st pw
ssk	sl2 kw 1 at a time, insert the left needle into the fronts of the 2 sts and knit together through the back loop [1 st decreased]
st(s)	stitch(es)
To wrap and turn (w+t) into a knit st:	insert right needle into the st below the st to be wrapped from right to left, lift that st and place it onto the left needle. Knit into the st just placed onto the left needle, then move the st being wrapped from the right to the left needle; you'll now have 2 sts coming out of the same st on the left needle. Turn to work the other direction - the 2 sts coming out of the single st count as 1 st when counting sts. When you are ready to knit the st with the wrap, knit the 2 sts of the wrapped st together.
To wrap and turn (w+t) into a purl st:	slip the st to be wrapped pw from the left needle to the right needle, and insert left needle into the st below the st to be wrapped from left to right. Lift the st and place it onto the left needle, then purl into the st you just placed onto the left needle; you'll now have 2 sts coming out of the same st on your right needle. Slip both sts pw to the left needle, and turn to work the other direction - the 2 sts coming out of the single st count as 1 st when counting sts. When you are ready to purl the st with the wrap, purl the 2 sts that are coming out of the single st together.
WS	wrong side
wyib	with yarn in back
yo	yarnover [1 st increased]

Difficulty Level

Easy   Intermediate   Advanced

For special technique tutorials, visit our website
javapurldesigns.com

Acknowledgements

From C.C.

To the Hubs, Russ, thank you times infinity for your never-ending support, encouragement, and love. Thank you for walking this journey with me. I love you the mostest-ostest-ostest!

To my daughter, Dami, thank you for your support, encouragement, and love. Thank you for co-hosting the podcast with me every single week, for sharing the love of knitting with me, and for being the model for so many of my photoshoots. I'm going to miss you so much when you go to SPU this autumn. You're my Lorelai Gilmore! I love you!

To my Great-Grandmother, Opal Cady, my Nana, Bertha Hobson, and my Momma, Beckey Wolfe, who crafted when I was a child and encouraged me to craft too.

To my bestie, Katy Kidwell, thank you for copy editing my book and for always being so excited about what I'm knitting now. You are the best friend I could ever hope for. I am so grateful for that random social media connection which brought our families together. Even though there's an ocean between us now, I love that we remain friends. Love you sweetie!

FROM DAMI

To my parents, both of whom inspire me on a daily basis, and to all the other creatives whom I've had the pleasure of admiring, whose work fills this grey world with every imaginable colour.

FROM US

To the amazing yarn dyers who dyed the yarn for this book, Neighborhood Fiber Co., Suburban Stitcher, Abstract Fiber, and Seven Sisters Arts, thank you for your creative colour genius that inspires us on a daily basis.

To our test knitters, Julia Bivens, Celeste Douville, Kimberly Napier, Kirsi Salmi, and Päivi Vauramo, thank you for finding our mistakes, advising us, and taking your time to knit our patterns.

To Rachel Brown of Porpoise Fur, thank you for being an amazing tech editor. You've taken our jumbled words and made them flow smoothly.

To the multitude of podcasters in the fibre world, thanks for keeping us company as we work. Special shout-outs to Jasmin and Gigi of The Knitmore Girls, Dianne of Suburban Stitcher, Rachel and Alli of Yarn in the City, and Tara of Explore Your Enthusiasm. Thank you for your support and friendship!

To Melissa Foltz for using your photographic magic to make our designs pop off the page. We're so grateful for you!

To the world of knitting designers, your creativity and brilliant patterns inspire us.

To the members of the Starship, thank you for celebrating our joys, offering support for our problems, and coming up with creative ideas to better our business.

To the viewers of the Geeky Girls Knit Podcast, thank you for journeying with us through our random, crazy, rambling weekly show. You are the best viewers podcasters could ever hope for.

To each person who has knit one or more of our patterns, thank you for taking our creativity and making it your own.

About C.C. & Dami

Hiya! I'm C.C. Almon. I'm half of the JavaPurl Designs / Geeky Girls Knit Podcast team. A little about me: I've been married for 20+ years to the love of my life Russ (aka The Hubs). I have a beautiful 18+ year old daughter Dami. We live in the Pacific Northwest.

I'm a self-taught knitter (began in 2005) and can crochet just enough to be dangerous. I began designing knitting patterns in 2012.

I'm addicted to coffee, the Gilmore Girls, Doctor Who, the colour pink, lots of geeky things, and knitting!

Hi, I'm Dami Almon!

I'm the other half of JavaPurl Designs and the Geeky Girls Knit podcast. I was taught to knit by my mom in 2007, and in recent years my love for it has only grown. I began designing patterns in 2016.

I'm in love with classic lit, Broadway (Great Comet! Hamilton!), a slew of geeky TV shows, and somewhat loosely consider myself an artist and writer.

Find Us Online

![javapurl - Hand Knit Designs Fueled by the Love of Coffee]

Website: JavaPurlDesigns.com
Email: grande@JavaPurlDesigns.com
Ravelry: JavaPurl | damisdoodles
Ravelry Group: JavaPurl Designs

Since 2012, we have co-hosted the weekly video podcast, Geeky Girls Knit.
Website: GeekyGirlsKnit.com
Ravelry Group: Geeky Girls Knit Podcast

www.ingramcontent.com/pod-product-compliance
Lightning Source LLC
Chambersburg PA
CBHW052238221025
34423CB00068B/4212